THE FUNNIEST IRELAND QUOTES... EVER!

Also available

The Funniest Liverpool Quotes... Ever!
The Funniest Chelsea Quotes... Ever!
The Funniest West Ham Quotes... Ever!
The Funniest Spurs Quotes... Ever!
The Funniest Arsenal Quotes... Ever!
The Funniest Man City Quotes... Ever!
The Funniest Newcastle Quotes... Ever!
The Funniest United Quotes... Ever!
The Funniest Celtic Quotes... Ever!
The Funniest QPR Quotes... Ever!
The Funniest Everton Quotes... Ever!
The Funniest Leeds Quotes... Ever!
The Funniest Rangers Quotes... Ever!
Mad All Over: The Funniest Crystal Palace Quotes... Ever!
Fergie Time: The Funniest Sir Alex Ferguson Quotes... Ever!
I Am The Normal One: The Funniest Jurgen Klopp Quotes... Ever!
I Didn't See It: The Funniest Arsene Wenger Quotes... Ever!
Zlatan Style: The Funniest Zlatan Ibrahimovic Quotes!
'Arry: The Funniest Harry Redknapp Quotes!
War of Words: The Funniest Neil Warnock Quotes!

THE FUNNIEST IRELAND QUOTES... EVER!

by Gordon Law

Copyright © 2020 by Eagle Books.

No part of this publication may be reproduced, stored in a retrieval system or transmitted in any form by any means, electronic, mechanical, photocopying, or otherwise, without prior written permission of the publisher Eagle Books.

contact@gmediagroup.co.uk

Printed in Europe and the USA.
ISBN: 978-1-917744-22-5
Imprint: Eagle Books

Photos courtesy of: Influential Photography/Shutterstock.com; John Gomez/Shutterstock.com; Joel Orme/Shutterstock.com

Contents

Introduction 6

Can You Manage? 9

Field Of Dreams 15

Sweet FAI 25

Calling The Shots 33

Game For a Laugh 43

Media Circus 51

Managing Just Fine 61

Talking Balls 71

Off The Pitch 81

Pundit Paradise 89

Fan Fever 99

Introduction

Everyone knows the Irish love a bit of the craic, so it's no surprise that the Ireland soccer team has given us loads of humorous sound bites.

Martin O'Neill always has something to say and is known as much for his comic quips as he is for his high energy on the touchline.

Whether it's a unique take on the game or a stinging put-down to a television pundit, O'Neill always comes up with the goods.

Like him or loathe him, Roy Keane is another colourful character who you can rely on to tell you how it is.

It's always a popcorn moment when he is taking a swipe at the modern-day footballer or blasting an underachieving teammate.

His most famous outburst was his fiery, yet hilarious rant at boss Mick McCarthy during the 2002 World Cup before he was sent home.

McCarthy's quick wit and brutal honesty is always entertaining, Jack Charlton's anecdotes are legendary and we can't forget the quirky comments from Giovanni Trapattoni.

Jason McAteer has produced some bloopers in his time, Tony Cascarino delivered some terrific tales, while Stephen Hunt's honest assessments were always amusing.

Many more rants and ramblings can be found in this unique collection of funny Ireland quotes and I hope you laugh as much reading this book as I did in compiling it.

Gordon Law

THE FUNNIEST IRELAND QUOTES... EVER!

CAN YOU MANAGE?

THE FUNNIEST IRELAND QUOTES... EVER!

"I have crossed the Alps barefoot and overcome most difficult situations in my career."
Giovanni Trapattoni says he can handle the pressure

"I won't die at a match. I might die being dragged down the River Tweed by a giant salmon, but a football match, no."
Jack Charlton

"I tell you one change that I've brought in is the use of DVDs of our opponents. That's a complete novelty for the Irish."
Giovanni Trapattoni

Can You Manage?

"What I learned from Jack [Charlton] – ensure that you're all inside the tent p*ssing out and get rid of any fellow who's outside the tent p*ssing in."
Mick McCarthy

Q: "Why do you remain confident the team will qualify for Euro 2020?"
A modest Martin O'Neill: "Because I'm good."

"I could be like the nice uncle, but only if we are winning. Everyone has an uncle they don't like, don't they?"
Roy Keane on his assistant manager role

THE FUNNIEST IRELAND QUOTES... EVER!

"I am the bad cop and he is the bad, bad cop."
Martin O'Neill on his assistant Roy Keane after being unveiled as manager

"I'm going to have to be the good cop compared to Martin. You don't know Martin as well as I do. He makes me look like Mother Teresa. I'm not some kind of animal."
Roy Keane responds

"We must remember that we have different material to work with – Italy have silk, whereas I only have cotton."
Giovanni Trapattoni

Can You Manage?

"I have to be coherent. There is a philosopher who says if you are too coherent, you run the risk of being an idiot but I can't keep changing."

Giovanni Trapattoni

"I felt like Tarzan."

Sir Bobby Robson gets into the swing of things on his first day as Ireland consultant

"Some managers have gone to tarot readers. But I am a believer and I believe in other things. Help yourself and God will help you. But I'm not God, I'm not St Patrick, I'm human."

Giovanni Trapattoni

THE FUNNIEST IRELAND QUOTES... EVER!

FIELD OF DREAMS

THE FUNNIEST IRELAND QUOTES... EVER!

"Something just hit me on the shoulder – I looked down and it was an open flick knife!"
Kevin Kilbane on an intimidating fixture in Georgia

"I told them when you lose, conceding one goal or six goals or three goals, it's the same."
Giovanni Trapattoni tries to play down a 6-1 loss to Germany

"On the pitch, the Italians looked no different to us. It was like playing Bournemouth on a wet Saturday."
Jason McAteer after Ireland's 1994 World Cup win

Field Of Dreams

"No regrets, none at all. My only regret is that we went out on penalties. That's my only regret. But no, no regrets."

Mick McCarthy after Ireland's 2002 World Cup exit

"For f*ck's sake, their anthem goes on, doesn't it? He looks at me and says, 'That's ours!'"

Terry Mancini to Don Givens on his debut

"Even Roy had said to him – Roy, of all people – 'Be careful'. And he said, 'I am, I am, I will be, I will be, I will be'. And then the Polish boy's legs were over the stand."

Martin O'Neill on James McClean

THE FUNNIEST IRELAND QUOTES... EVER!

"As the first bars ring out, I notice the TV camera starts to zoom in. Should I move my lips and sing the two or three lines that I know?"
Andy Townsend on the national anthem

"I think the goalkeeper went for the sod of grass Cas kicked as the ball bobbled under him."
Mick McCarthy on Tony Cascarino's penalty against Romania at Italia 90

"There are moments a coach needs to take a stone and throw it at the water so that – boom! Everything changes."
Giovanni Trapattoni on why he used early substitutions against Italy

Field Of Dreams

"When the golden goal went in it was like doing 10 years in prison and then walking out and getting a smack off a bus."

Ireland U20 boss Gerry Smith after his team were defeated by Colombia

"In the dressing room after the game, Jack Charlton thanked us all and his final words were, 'We've had a great World Cup, we've had a great time, go and have great holidays... Oh and by the way Packie, the Pope would have saved that!'"

Tony Cascarino on Jack Charlton's message to Packie Bonner after his mistake led to their Italia 90 exit

THE FUNNIEST IRELAND QUOTES... EVER!

"We should have scored a few more goals, six is better than five, seven is better than six, eight would have been better than seven."
Bobby Robson after Ireland's 5-0 win over San Marino

"I'm happy we beat them and played them here [in Germany]. I hope that the Russians pull out now... hehe... and they get to play the rest of their matches at home."
Stephen Hunt after Ireland beat Georgia

"I thought their keeper Van der Sar was like a 13th man."
Steve Staunton after losing 4-0 to Holland

Field Of Dreams

"I thought, I've fallen for it. I've fallen for the big one. [The two burly men in the front] are going to do me. Jaysus, how's it going to finish? Will they kill me here in the woods? In the end the scam was they wanted $50 instead of $20. I was never so happy just to be ripped off."

Eoin Hand gets stung by a taxi driver while scouting for Brian Kerr at a Georgia vs Moldova game in Tbilisi

"One day you're the greatest thing since sliced bread when you're knocking the goals in. But if you go a few games without a goal, suddenly you're a w*nker."

Don Givens

THE FUNNIEST IRELAND QUOTES... EVER!

"I think I've had only a couple of bookings in the last dozen games, which is good for me. I had better not say any more or I'll probably be sent off tonight."

And he was... Roy Keane before his red card against Russia

"I can't pass the ball for them."

Steve Staunton takes a swipe at his players after a draw with Cyprus

"I wanted to kill a few of them last night but I've moved on from that."

Assistant manager Roy Keane after a home defeat by Belarus

Field Of Dreams

"We came in at half-time, one-up, and realised that a dog had got into the dressing room and he'd sh*t on the floor. The last one in is Gilesy. He walks in, steps over it and says, 'Ah, who's sh*t on the floor?' I put my hand up and said, 'Me, but I'm good in the air'."

Terry Mancini on his debut against Poland

"Don't jump the gun. In Italy it is other meaning but the same. Be careful the cat, no say the cat is in the sack when you have not the cat in the sack."

Giovanni Trapattoni ahead of the Euro 2012 second leg play-off against Estonia with Ireland leading 4-0

THE FUNNIEST IRELAND QUOTES... EVER!

SWEET FAI

THE FUNNIEST IRELAND QUOTES... EVER!

Reporter: "It's been said that your weakness is that you have never played at the highest level."

Brian Kerr: "Well, I don't think the FAI has hired me as a player – they've hired me as a manager."

"At one stage, I was involved in a discussion which centered on a flight plan around cruise missile attack paths. They seemed to know where the missiles were coming from."

An Irish FA official on negotiations with UEFA about postponing the Macedonia v Ireland game during the Kosovo crisis

Sweet FAI

"The Irish football story goes back 70 years and it's a thread that incompetence and stupid administration has robbed Irish football. There is a poverty of aspiration and poverty of expectation. I want a bleeding revolution."
Eamon Dunphy

"You'd get some real potato pickers coming out to play. A selector with a bit of clout would want to pick some of his boys. You have a League of Ireland player capped and right away he's worth a few thousand quid."
Charlie Hurley

THE FUNNIEST IRELAND QUOTES... EVER!

"Joe Wickham used to phone you or you got a letter to say you were selected. The itinerary would tell you to bring your own soap, your own towel, your own everything."

Noel Cantwell on the FAI

"Hotel's been great, the food's been lovely, the training ground is lovely – no potholes, we've footballs, there's even bibs. Major progress."

A smiling No.2 Roy Keane in rare praise for the FAI

"I have a perfect relationship with these guys, they love me and I hate them."

Liam Tuohy on the FAI in 1972

Sweet FAI

"The FAI do their business in mysterious ways. It's smoke and mirrors stuff... the majority of them you wouldn't trust to mind your corner shop for 10 minutes."
Brian Kerr

"Good luck at the World Cup. By the way, any chance of a ticket?"
Eoin Hand to England's Ron Greenwood after the FAI hadn't got him a seat

"It's unfortunate that I've been personally linked with the appointment."
FAI chief executive John Delaney refuses to take the blame for appointing Steve Staunton

THE FUNNIEST IRELAND QUOTES... EVER!

Reporter: "Any preferences on who Bertie's successor should be?"

Roy Keane (as Sunderland manager): "John Delaney?"

"If I'm trying to distract from Sunderland's results that would be very hard to do because they were that bad. I would have to give the press conferences naked to take the attention off the results."

John Delaney responds to Keane's comment

"Where we trained in Clonshaugh was abysmal and it has been for as long as I've known it."

Roy Keane – years before the Saipan incident

Sweet FAI

"They would put Johnny Giles and Joe Haverty into size 44 shorts. In the dressing room, sometimes they'd pull the shorts over their heads."
Noel Cantwell on the FAI messing up the playing kit sizes

"If I was John Delaney, I say Giovanni continue because Giovanni make great job."
Giovanni Trapattoni when asked if his position was safe

"Certainly the chief executive can't play on an international football pitch and score goals, if I could I'd love to."
John Delaney

THE FUNNIEST IRELAND QUOTES... EVER!

CALLING THE SHOTS

THE FUNNIEST IRELAND QUOTES... EVER!

"Well he didn't have the baby, did he? Unless he's breastfeeding he should be alright."
Roy Keane when asked if Robbie Keane would be available for selection despite his wife being pregnant

"I watched you two years ago and you were cr*p. Do you want to come and play for Ireland?"
Jack Charlton to Tony Cascarino

"I love Kevin Doyle. As a player, not as a man. I love women, without a doubt."
Giovanni Trapattoni

Calling The Shots

"I have never had to listen to such a foul-mouthed abuse from any footballer in any dressing room or any meeting room. I have never witnessed such an attack from any human being in any walk of life."

Mick McCarthy on the infamous clash with Roy Keane at the 2002 World Cup

"As he waded in with one expletive after another, I asked myself if this was my captain. Was this a man who could serve Ireland as a role model for our children? The answer was no."

Mick McCarthy after Roy Keane's rant in Japan

THE FUNNIEST IRELAND QUOTES... EVER!

"I think you're going far too far up the road now for James [McClean] to be captain of the side – he's a lunatic!"
Martin O'Neill

"I like [David] Meyler, I signed him. One of my better signings... but that wouldn't have been hard."
Assistant manager Roy Keane

"You were f*cking cr*p!"
Jack Charlton tells Tony Cascarino why he was dropped after a poor display in training

Calling The Shots

"I don't forget Lee Carsley... OK, so Carsley is now on a pension."

Giovanni Trapattoni

"I used to fall out with Mr Clough, but we won European Cups."

Martin O'Neill on Harry Arter's confrontation with Roy Keane

"I'm not going to drive up to Manchester to be humiliated by someone like that."

Don Givens on trying to coax Stephen Ireland back into the squad

THE FUNNIEST IRELAND QUOTES... EVER!

"For me, it's not closed. I hope something can happen in the future. In other categories, the great champions, they come back. A great example is Schumacher and Tyson. OK, maybe for money. Schumacher not for money. Tyson? Maybe."
Giovanni Trapattoni on Stephen Ireland returning from international exile

"Anyone who used the word 'quintessentially' in a half-time talk is talking cr*p."
Mick McCarthy on Niall Quinn

"He jumps like a kangaroo."
Giovanni Trapattoni on Shane Long

Calling The Shots

"I tucked Duffer up tight last night with a few DVDs and some Mikado biscuits I brought with me from back home."

Brian Kerr helps Damien Duff to sleep

Jack Charlton: "Bloody hell, Maurice. We haven't picked that lanky buggah... have we?"
Maurice Setters: "Think we had to."
Niall Quinn overhears his manager as he walks into the hotel reception

"I don't watch Twitter."
Giovanni Trapattoni reacts to a James McClean tweet

THE FUNNIEST IRELAND QUOTES... EVER!

"Stephen [Ireland] is not my son and I cannot force him to play. If you want to try to force him, do. You pray, I no. Will he come back? Maybe."
Giovanni Trapattoni

"The more you talk about it, the worse it is. He will read what I say in the paper and he closes up like a hedgehog."
Giovanni Trapattoni on Stephen Ireland coming back to the squad

"A boring old sh*te."
Jack Charlton's tribute to Denis Irwin at the player's testimonial dinner

Calling The Shots

Ray Houghton: "I'm the only one getting the chances!"

Jack Charlton: "You're the only one missing the chances."

A touchline exchange after the midfielder was taken off during the 1994 World Cup qualifier against Northern Ireland

"He talks a good game. Imagine if he'd won a trophy. He goes on the TV about how he was harshly treated by me."

Roy Keane on Jonathan Walters

"He is built like a wardrobe."

Giovanni Trapattoni on Richard Dunne

THE FUNNIEST IRELAND QUOTES... EVER!

GAME FOR A LAUGH

THE FUNNIEST IRELAND QUOTES... EVER!

"I wouldn't watch a whole England game but I see the highlights."

Roy Keane

"David Bentley is David Bentley – he ain't bloody Maradona. He plays for England and hype comes with England. People don't go on about Damien Duff and Robbie Keane every day so they need to get a life."

Stephen Hunt

Tony Cascarino: "Who the f*ck is that?"
Niall Quinn: "Shut up, it's the Taoiseach."
When Charles Haughey entered the dressing room after Ireland's Italia 90 exit

"I just hope everything will be OK because it is in the back of your mind that anything you do, you could pick up something."

Stephen McPhail on an U20s trip to Nigeria

"Why should we go and chase people? We are f*cking Ireland."

Robbie Keane on players choosing to play for the Boys in Green

"We need to get some top players coming through but having watched the U21s a few weeks ago I wouldn't get my hopes up too high."

Roy Keane

THE FUNNIEST IRELAND QUOTES... EVER!

"Packie [Bonner] said that they'd worked hard. Alan [Kelly] said that they'd worked hard. I said, 'Do you want a pat on the back for working hard – is that not why we are here?' I did mention that they wouldn't be too tired to play golf the next day, and fair play, they dragged themselves out."
Roy Keane on the goalkeeping row at the 2002 World Cup

"What's up with me? What's up with me? We're f*cking playing Holland tomorrow in a World Cup qualifier. Do you think Jimmy Floyd-Hasselbaink is eating f*cking cheese sandwiches tonight?"
Roy Keane

"And when he got on the bus and started staring at the roof I knew we were heading for trouble."

Jason McAteer on the prelude to Roy Keane's bust-up at the 2002 World Cup

"Dean Kiely [Ireland's reserve goalkeeper] is one of the quieter lads in the group. 'I'd like to say something, Mick,' he said. We all turned and looked at him. 'If you want, I can do a job for you in midfield'. And the place just erupted!"

Jason McAteer in the immediate aftermath of the Saipan row

THE FUNNIEST IRELAND QUOTES... EVER!

"National teams don't interest me. I have more to do than go off for three days to play Andorra. And when you are Irish, you are well aware you'll never win the World Cup."

Stephen Ireland

"Dave [O'Leary] was all right, yeah, not that he was a big mate of mine, nobody was."

Roy Keane

"[We need] someone who is honest and someone who has balls. Someone who doesn't take any sh*t from anybody."

Robbie Keane on Giovanni Trapattoni's successor

Game For a Laugh

"If GAA players tried to live with the level of commitment shown by a professional footballer, they wouldn't know what hit them."

Stephen Hunt fires shots at the GAA stars

"I know the beginning, Sinne Fianna Fail, and that's all I know, and that's what I used to do. I'd stand at the front, because I know the cameras would come on at the front, and then it would go across. It's good innit?"

Clinton Morrison on singing the Irish national anthem

"I was more nervous in training than in games."

Alan McLoughlin at Italia 90

THE FUNNIEST IRELAND QUOTES... EVER!

MEDIA CIRCUS

THE FUNNIEST IRELAND QUOTES... EVER!

"These guys are entitled to their opinion. They've played at a decent level. Well, two of them have played at a decent level."

Roy Keane on criticism by RTE pundits Liam Brady, Johnny Giles and Eamon Dunphy

"Can we go now please? I'd like a beer."

Jack Charlton to the media after a 3-0 loss to Portugal

Journalist: "Where did it go wrong?"
Steve Staunton: "The five goals."
After a 5-2 defeat to Cyprus

Media Circus

"If I was listening at all to your punditry team, there would be little chance of us fighting back. But thankfully I didn't listen to them and particularly a couple, who should possibly be looking for other jobs themselves now, because they get it wrong so often."
Martin O'Neill takes a swipe at the RTE pundits

Reporter: "What happened to the team bus?"
Mick McCarthy: "It broke down."
Reporter: "Can you expand on that?"
McCarthy: "It wouldn't go any further."
Press conference exchange after Ireland's 2-0 win over Gibraltar

THE FUNNIEST IRELAND QUOTES... EVER!

"I know you. You are a trouble maker... I'm bigger than you."
Jack Charlton to Eamon Dunphy at his first press conference as manager

"In his interviews, [David] Beckham manages to sit on the fence very well and keeps both ears on the ground."
Brian Kerr

Reporter: "The [Prague] pitch looks good?"
Lee Carsley: "Yeah, no bobbles... but I'll find one."
The midfielder isn't confident about his first touch ahead of the game against the Czechs

Media Circus

"If you write one bad article, does your editor say, 'OK, you are out' because of one bad article? I think no."
Giovanni Trapattoni

Q: "What's your tactical plans for the game?"
Steve Staunton: "Well, Shay Given in goal, four at the back, four in midfield and two up front."

"Maybe that's why he only managed eight games, that might be something to do with it."
Martin O'Neill questions Alan Shearer after he criticised Cyrus Christie's Fulham display

THE FUNNIEST IRELAND QUOTES... EVER!

"It's been way over the top. I haven't murdered anyone. No courses could have taught me what I've had to go through."
Steve Staunton on coping with the flak

Journalist: "You look tense tonight, Mick."
Mick McCarthy: "You want to try sitting in the dugout when it's your a*se in the bacon slicer."
After Ireland's 2002 World Cup clash with Saudi Arabia

"That's propaganda, that's like going over to Russia 50 years ago."
Steve Staunton denies Irish fans booed the team off the pitch in San Marino

"Football's answer to Andy Capp."

Eamon Dunphy on Jack Charlton

"I'm not a thick ignorant Andy Capp Geordie, I won't answer to that. I do a professional job... I was asked to do a job for the Irish and I did it the way I felt needed to be done."

Charlton's response to Dunphy

"My refusal to answer questions from Dunphy was the biggest mistake I ever made. I made Eamon very, very famous."

Charlton on facing off with the journalist and TV pundit

THE FUNNIEST IRELAND QUOTES... EVER!

"You want me to compete with the best in the world, I've got to have the f*cking best in the world. And it's not here in Ireland that I can find it, I've got to go to England to find it, or Scotland... Now if you don't want to do that, tell me, and I'll f*cking concentrate on the League of Ireland and we'll win nothing."
Jack Charlton snaps at a journalist

"If you get a bad defeat, a poor performance, then it's like a turkey shoot. But there's only one target and everyone is standing there facing you with a machine gun."
Steve Staunton on press conferences

Media Circus

"Just before we did our interview you said to me, 'Hard luck' – just before we went on air. What did you mean by that? You weren't being disingenuous about it were you?"

Martin O'Neill puts RTE's Tony O'Donoghue in his place after the 5-1 World Cup play-off loss to Denmark

"Where do they get their kicks from? Do you know what I mean? And especially [Eamon] Dunphy, he should know better by now. He's a skinny rat, a skinny little rat."

Stephen Hunt responds to the pundit's criticism of a 2-2 draw with Italy

THE FUNNIEST IRELAND QUOTES... EVER!

MANAGING JUST FINE

THE FUNNIEST IRELAND QUOTES... EVER!

"They're difficult to break down."

Steve Staunton on the mighty San Marino

"We're the team that doesn't study the opposition, that takes supporters on the team coach, is not really bothered, that likes a pint and the craic. And yet here we are in the last 16 of the World Cup again. If that scenario were true, we must be the greatest group of guys who ever played the game."

Mick McCarthy

"A win is a win if you win it."

Steve Staunton on beating the Czechs

Managing Just Fine

"We're from Ireland, not the bloody Gobi desert."

Jack Charlton before the 1994 World Cup clash in the scorching heat of Orlando

"It was suggested by him. At first I thought, 'You cheeky b*llocks."

Mick McCarthy on Robbie Keane wanting to coach in the Irish set-up

"He has been a great player and had great success. I don't know if he achieved the same results as coach or manager."

Giovanni Trapattoni hits back at comments from Roy Keane

THE FUNNIEST IRELAND QUOTES... EVER!

"I'll buy Bryan Hamilton a bottle of whisky – duty free because it costs less."

Jack Charlton owes the Northern Ireland manager after victory over Austria keeps the Republic's Euro hopes alive

"I just want a solid team with a good balance that plays international football – like this table, with its legs, you have to be solid."

Giovanni Trapattoni

"We probably got on better with the likes of Holland, Belgium, Norway and Sweden, some of whom are not even European."

Jack Charlton

Managing Just Fine

"I didn't break his nose. Not at all. He ran away too quick. I couldn't catch him."

Noel King on an alleged Shamrock Rovers training ground row with Eamon Dunphy

"I went to a game at Hull where most of the Irish lads were on the bench. Paul McShane made the point, 'Well I hope you watched the warm-up!'."

Assistant manager Roy Keane

"I have eight very good defenders in my squad, nine if you include Gary Doherty."

Bryan Kerr

THE FUNNIEST IRELAND QUOTES... EVER!

"I always felt the Everton players were going to turn up on crutches or crawling in the hotel door. Maybe they're overloading players with games, but that usually means you're playing midweek games and Everton don't do that because they don't play European football."

Roy Keane has a dig at Everton's Ronald Koeman over James McCarthy's fitness

"He would join my to-call list, but I should first put a call in to Trump to congratulate him. And then give my commiserations to Hillary. Then somewhere down the line, Koeman."

Martin O'Neill on lining up a chat with Koeman about the McCarthy issue

"Sending that tw*t home."

Mick McCarthy on the highlight of his first spell as boss. Roy Keane, if you wondered

"He's fine. We locked him up about 25 minutes ago. He's caged in at this minute, as his beard gets longer, and uglier. But he's good. He's the werewolf of Manchester."

Martin O'Neill on his 'scary' assistant Roy Keane

"If, in winning the game, we only end up with a draw, we would be fine."

Jack Charlton

THE FUNNIEST IRELAND QUOTES... EVER!

"I like Keith but do you know what, I have to turn around and say that's complete b*llocks. It is honestly, it is complete and utter b*llocks."
Martin O'Neill after Keith Andrews claimed Ireland got a lucky play-off draw. He said: "At the moment, if Martin fell in muck, he'd still smell of Old Spice. He's got that at the moment so I wasn't surprised at the draw."

"I'm not a magician, I can't see where they all are. Maybe two or three come back after the rest, the day after the off-day, with problem. Drink beer. Go with wife. Happen [to be an] accident. I hope not."
Giovanni Trapattoni on players' time off

Managing Just Fine

Q: "Is it an advantage that Christian Eriksen is playing a Champions League final five days before Denmark play you?"

Mick McCarthy: "Only if somebody clumps him I guess."

"I'm sure a lot of the players probably don't particularly like me."

Assistant manager Roy Keane

"There are only two certainties in life: people die and football managers get the sack."

Eoin Hand

THE FUNNIEST IRELAND QUOTES... EVER!

TALKING BALLS

THE FUNNIEST IRELAND QUOTES... EVER!

"He's probably not been interviewed yet, the new fella, so f*ck knows."

Damien Duff when asked if he thought the new manager watched Ireland's last game

"There's something about Jack Charlton that makes me want to play for him. He could [even] be the manager of Swaziland."

Jason McAteer

"He doesn't realise I'm Irish, even though I've played 67 times, scored 11 goals and am the second leading scorer in the squad."

Ian Harte on Giovanni Trapattoni

Talking Balls

"If ever a player was out of his class that night, it was me."

Eamon Dunphy on his Ireland debut

"I looked at him and I thought, 'He's a big guy. This guy can't move'. In training, we had 11 v 11, and the ball has gone down the side, and he cleaned me and the ball and everything and put me basically over the hedges. It was an unbelievable tackle."

Clinton Morrison on Richard Dunne

"Stephen Hunt's international career didn't really pull up many trees."

James McClean on Stephen Hunt. Ouch!

THE FUNNIEST IRELAND QUOTES... EVER!

"Roy lives in Roy Keane World and refuses to accept other people's autonomy or opinion."
Matt Holland

"I have got big legs and a big backside – it's just the way I am, I will always have a big a*se. I can't get rid of that."
David Dunn

"If he left everybody out of the squad who was singing that night, there'd probably be only two people in the squad – and that's only because they didn't know the songs we were singing."
Andy Reid was axed by Giovanni Trapattoni after late-night hotel sing-song

Talking Balls

Q: "What is the funniest thing you've ever seen on a football pitch?"
Liam Miller: "Stephen Hunt's hair."

"Jack used to go around to pubs in Ireland and pay with cheques rather than cash. No one would cash it, they would get it framed and put it behind the bar instead, so it worked out that he never paid for anything."
Paul McGrath on Jack Charlton

"Roy Keane? He says enough anyway. I played with him at Celtic and that was bad enough."
Aiden McGeady

THE FUNNIEST IRELAND QUOTES... EVER!

"Who do you think you are having meetings about me? You were a cr*p player and you are a cr*p manager. The only reason I have any dealings with you is that somehow you are the manager of my country and you're not even Irish, you English c*nt!"

Roy Keane blasts Mick McCarthy at the 2002 World Cup

"A flowerpot."

Eamon Dunphy describes Ray Treacy

"Obviously I bother him a little bit, he doesn't bother me one single bit."

Jonathan Walters hits out at Roy Keane

Talking Balls

"He called me James to begin with and stuck with it. The funny thing is I started responding to the name."
Paul McGrath on Jack Charlton

"He was big, he was blunt, he was English."
Niall Quinn on Jack Charlton's arrival

"After that we had a chat and I guess he shouldn't have to sell it to me. But I think he should have made some sort of effort to sell it to me."
Stephen Ireland on Giovanni Trapattoni discussing his international future

THE FUNNIEST IRELAND QUOTES... EVER!

"Jack Charlton's first words to me were, 'You're number eight, Ian'. I said, 'Ian Brady was the Moors murderer, Jack'."
Liam Brady

"I am one for tackling things head on, so when we next bump into each other, I will have it out with him."
Tony Cascarino after Shay Given questioned his Irishness

"Robbie Brady, you absolute ride."
Shane Lowry tweets his appreciation after the winger's goal against Italy. Ride?

Talking Balls

"I'd rather buy a Bob the Builder CD for my two-year-old than Roy Keane's book."

Jason McAteer

"Jack [Charlton] had beseeched our captain Mick McCarthy to 'Stay tight on Van Cleef'. Mick had to tell Jack that Lee van Cleef was a dead Hollywood film star."

Alan McLoughlin on the World Cup game against Holland

"Eamon [Dunphy] was reading those strange books. He seemed to get into some very intellectual books."

Joe Kinnear on his room mate

THE FUNNIEST IRELAND QUOTES... EVER!

OFF THE PITCH

THE FUNNIEST IRELAND QUOTES... EVER!

"[Curtis Fleming] is teaching me how to speak a bit of Irish and drink Guinness. I'm struggling. I only really know how to drink Guinness."
Clinton Morrison

"I'll have it in four, I would never eat eight."
Jason McAteer on how many slices he likes his pizza cut into

"I got quite handy at capturing white rats on the floor. Overall I thought it was good training for managing in the League of Ireland!"
Brian Kerr worked as a lab technician with the Department of Agriculture

Off The Pitch

"I saw the players eating mushrooms before a friendly, I was stunned into silence for several seconds."

Giovanni Trapattoni

"We go into Malahide and have a coffee, it's fine. We were out last night for a meal, it was fine. We're not One Direction."

No.2 Roy Keane

"It's not unusual for me to be standing at a bar and a pint of beer will appear in front of me, and I've already got one."

Jack Charlton

THE FUNNIEST IRELAND QUOTES... EVER!

"One of his cardinals introduced us, saying, 'This is Mr Charlton'. The Pope said, 'Ah yes, the boss'."

Jack Charlton on his squad's Vatican trip

"The Pope was smaller than I expected, but only in size."

Jack Charlton

"The Pope was on the third bit of his blessing and he was looking right at me and he had his hand in the air like that (raises hand). As I woke up, I thought he was waving at me so I stood up and waved back at him."

Jack Charlton nodded off during the service

Off The Pitch

"The amount of fights I've had in Cork would probably be another book. I mean, people go on about my problems off the field, but they don't even know the half of it."
Roy Keane

"Damien has been known to suffer from time to time from, eh, adhesive mattress syndrome."
Brian Kerr on Damien Duff liking his sleep

"Italy turn up in Armani suits looking the dog's b*llocks and we arrive in bright green blazers and dodgy brogues."
Phil Babb on the 1994 World Cup

THE FUNNIEST IRELAND QUOTES... EVER!

"It's a good test, isn't it?"

Steve Staunton after being threatened by a man brandishing a gun at the team's hotel

"Well, it depends on how good looking the girls are. If they are really attractive, they're very, very welcome. The uglier ones, I'm afraid not."

Martin O'Neill when asked if the WAGs could visit the team hotel at Euro 2016

"What are you drinking that sh*t for? Guinness is better for you."

Jack Charlton to any of his players if he caught them drinking Coke

Off The Pitch

"I do it at home, as well, strolling around like Tarzan in just a pair of Nikes. The neighbours know me pretty well."

Gary Kelly on walking around his hotel room naked

"Jimmy White, 180!"

Jason McAteer when the snooker player walked into a Dublin pub

"Football is concrete. We are not a theatre, La Scala or Madison Square Garden – it's football."

Giovanni Trapattoni

THE FUNNIEST IRELAND QUOTES... EVER!

PUNDIT PARADISE

THE FUNNIEST IRELAND QUOTES... EVER!

"The best thing for [Ireland] to do is to stay at 0-0 until they score the goal."

Martin O'Neill

"I might be tempting fate but I can't see the Poles scoring... Oh noooo... they just have!"

George Hamilton

"Would you let him drive the train to Cork?"

Eamon Dunphy on Steve Staunton

"Kilbane did what he normally does: ran his heart out and gave the ball away a lot."

Johnny Giles

Pundit Paradise

"Ireland have won a corner, and it's in a very good position."

George Hamilton

"Usually it takes a bottle of Bacardi and a gallon of Coke to get John out of his seat."

Eamon Dunphy on Johnny Giles

"His reign ended with that 0-0 defeat by Switzerland at Lansdowne Road."

Colm Murray on Brian Kerr

"McLean's been like a fresh of breath air."

Roy Keane

THE FUNNIEST IRELAND QUOTES... EVER!

Eamon Dunphy: "Just think of the Irish children crying going to their beds last night."

Vincent Browne: "But Eamon, what about the happy children in Norway?"

The pundits react after Ireland's loss

"We don't really know what Iran are capable of when the gun is put to their head."

George Hamilton on Ireland's World Cup play-off opponents

Bill O'Herlihy: "[Lee] Carsley lacks a bit of skill in those situations. Let's call a spade a spade."

Johnny Giles: "Yes Bill, he's in there to dig."

Pundit Paradise

"James McCarthy is a talking horse. Horses that produce the goods on the gallops in the morning, but never do it on the racecourse."
Eamon Dunphy

"[The fans] were swizzed out of an international match."
Brian Kerr on reserves playing in the Ireland v Iceland friendly

"The flags are waving, and no doubt at the foot of the Alps, the cow bells are chiming too. And it's going to take a lot for Ireland to turn it round and sour the chocolate."
George Hamilton on a clash with Switzerland

THE FUNNIEST IRELAND QUOTES... EVER!

"Kilbane's head is better than his feet. If only he had three heads, one on the end of each leg."
Eamon Dunphy

"Jack [Charlton] is not always right, but he is never wrong."
Johnny Giles

"Ireland will give 99 per cent – everything they've got."
Mark Lawrenson

"Let's hope that's a surgical staple gun."
George Hamilton on Richard Dunne's injury

Pundit Paradise

"Glum oranges. In fact I think the fruit their feelings are more akin to is a lemon."

George Hamilton on Ireland's victory over Holland

Q: "Are Ireland favourites for the game against Belgium?"

Roy Keane: "Have you been drinking?"

The pundit at Euro 2016

George Hamilton: "Roy Carsley has it."

Jim Magee: "Lee Carsley, George."

Hamilton: "Ah yes, perhaps it's because his head reminds me of Ray Wilkins."

THE FUNNIEST IRELAND QUOTES... EVER!

"Ireland don't have the players they used to – the O'Learys, the Stapletons, the Bradys."
David O'Leary

"Niall Quinn is a creep. The man's an idiot, a Mother Teresa."
Eamon Dunphy

"It's 57 goals for Robbie Keane and 57 varieties of goal."
George Hamilton

"Ireland need fresh impotence."
Phil Babb

Pundit Paradise

"He was like a drunken gambler in a casino. He was throwing chips on the table. Noel Hunt for Kevin Doyle – are you serious? Folan for Keogh – are you serious?"
Eamon Dunphy on Giovanni Trapattoni after a draw against 10-man Italy

"I wouldn't know Brian Kerr from a bar of soap."
Rodney Marsh

"The seeds of doubt that were sown at the weekend against Egypt have been doused by a dose of Jack Charlton's almighty weedkiller."
George Hamilton at Italia 90

THE FUNNIEST IRELAND QUOTES... EVER!

FAN FEVER

THE FUNNIEST IRELAND QUOTES... EVER!

"Alive, alive-o-oh. Alive, alive-o-oh. Stephen Ireland's two grannies. Alive, alive-oh!"

A song for the midfielder after he pretended one granny, then the other was dead to excuse himself from playing

"Don't blame it on Staunton, don't blame it on Givens, don't blame it on Keano, blame it on Delaney."

Chant at FAI chief executive John Delaney, to the tune of Blame it on the Boogie

"Ooh aah Paul McGrath's da!"

Nelson Mandela's memorable ditty when he visited Ireland

Fan Fever

"He's shagging your wife. He's shagging your wife. Jan Vertonghen, he's shagging your wife!"
Ireland fans taunt Christian Eriksen during their match against Denmark

"We've got Wesley, Wesley Hoolahan, I just don't think you understand. The super Irish man, he's better than Zidane, we've got Wesley Hoolahan."
Irish fans' tribute to the midfielder

"Go home to your sexy wives, go home to your sexy wives!"
Banter with the Swedish fans at Euro 2016, to the tune of Go West by the Pet Shop Boys

THE FUNNIEST IRELAND QUOTES... EVER!

"He is Ward, he is Ward. He has risen from the dead and he is Ward. Every cross he makes, every heart he breaks. Jesus Christ is Ward."

A Stephen Ward song to the tune of the church hymn He is Lord, He is Lord

"We've got Glenn Whelan, and tonight's gonna be a good night!"

Whelan gets his own song, to the tune of I've Got A Feeling by The Black Eyed Peas

"He wears a tea cosy on his head, he's got a big tea cosy on his head."

The Boys in Green salute Stephen Hunt in Prague against the Czechs

Fan Fever

"All you need is Duff, da da da da da. All you need is Duff, da da da da da. All you need is Duff, Duff. Duff is all you need."

Damien Duff gets a catchy song to the tune of The Beatles' All You Need is Love

"Oh Trapattoni. He used to be Italian but he's Irish now. Oh Trapattoni. He used to be Italian but he's Irish now..."

The supporters get behind their manager

"Who needs Capello, we've got our Trappo. Who needs Capello, we've got our Trappo!"

The fans would take Trapattoni ahead of England's Fabio Capello any day

THE FUNNIEST IRELAND QUOTES... EVER!

www.ingramcontent.com/pod-product-compliance
Lightning Source LLC
Chambersburg PA
CBHW071126130526
44590CB00056B/2464